Family
Changes

Aspiring Families Press
12625 High Bluff Drive, Ste. 104
San Diego, CA 92130
www.AspiringFamiliesPress.com

Book Cover & Interior by Advocate Art
and Monkey C Media

Printed in the United States of America

ISBN-13: 978-0-9961941-0-5
LCCN: 2014918463

For
PAIGE and KIMBERLEY

Note to Adults

Divorce is a significant but common stressor that could influence a child's emotional wellbeing. This book will allow you and your child to safely approach feelings and questions and create a common language to understand the family changes. As a clinical psychologist with twenty years of expertise in child development, my best recommendation to divorcing parents is to be mindful of and responsive to their child's emotional needs. This book will thoughtfully guide you to help your child cope effectively during a potentially difficult transition.

Family Changes enables parents and other significant adults (teachers, therapists, grandparents, and caregivers) to explain factual and emotional information related to separation and divorce with children (ages 4–8 years). The story identifies and normalizes young children's feelings, concerns, and questions about divorce. Feelings of sadness, anxiety, loss, confusion, and anger are highlighted for the child via safe adults, peers, and the fantasy of a story.

Storytelling can be an effective technique for therapists and other adults to share complicated information, and to explore children's difficult feelings and questions. It gives children a new understanding and new ways to talk about their feelings without shame, blame, criticism, or guilt. Also, adults often struggle with explaining and comforting children through the fears, anxiety, and unknowns that are part of life changes. This book will help you and other important adults, connect with your child and encourage your child to trust you.

The story emphasizes that with children, moving between play, process, and fantasy is an effective mechanism to work through anxiety provoking content. The theme of "it's happening to them and not to me" in the story makes it safe for the young child to have an ongoing dialogue at different times in the day, rather than having a one-time "sit-down discussion."

A list of questions offered at the end of the book enables the adult to work with the child at a deeper level. This interactive piece is vital, as it allows the child to focus on his or her own thoughts and feelings and allows for an active dialogue with an adult.

Though *Family Changes* does not provide a magical solution nor simple resolution; it suggests that understanding and coping with divorce is likely to be a longer-term developmental process and not a one-time conversation. Importantly, the story brings the child hope and the possibility that happiness and a positive family life can exist in two homes.

The task of explaining divorce to a young child can be daunting: my hope is that my book will allow you to do to this in a safe, effective, and healthy way that will keep your child feeling positive, connected, and secure.

Family Changes

Today was a big day at the Sunny Bunny School. Today was special because the school was having a treasure hunt with magical prizes and hop dancing.

"Morning, honey bunny," Mama Bunny whispered, kissing Zoey on the top of her long, velvety ears.

"Yaaaawwwn," smiled Zoey, rubbing her big brown eyes. She had been dreaming about chocolate carrots and ice cream lettuce at the treasure hunt. But, as she thought more about it, Zoey realized that a word kept popping up in her dreams. The word was "SEPARATE" and it made her feel worried.

As Zoey shook her head clear of her fuzzy dreams, she decided she would ask Mama about the word in her dreams. Zoey whispered, "Mama, what does SEPARATE mean?"

"Why do you ask what SEPARATE means, little one?" asked Mama Bunny.

"Well", said Zoey, "I keep thinking of the word in my dreams. I also heard you tell Granny Bunny, that Daddy and you are SEPARATED now. You also say DIVORCE a lot. Do SEPARATE and DIVORCE go together?"

"Those are big questions for such a little bunny like you, Zoey. But I will explain as best I can. SEPARATE means when two married people choose to live in two different homes. DIVORCE also means when two married people decide to live in two different homes, but for a long, long time. Usually forever."

"Oh..." said Zoey with a quiet nod. Her stomach began to hurt a little, and her velvety ears drooped. She hopped to the bathroom to get ready for school. As Zoey brushed her shiny, big teeth, she began to dream about the treasure hunt again. She thought about finding the Magic Silver Ball that bounced eight feet high and the Glittering Feather that flew on its own. Zoey became so excited that her ears began to wiggle up and down and side to side, and her nose just wouldn't stop twitching.

Zoey quickly dressed for school and hop-hop-hopped out of the house with Mama Bunny trying to keep up behind her. As Mama was dropping Zoey off at school in their bunny go-kart, Zoey's stomach began to hurt again, and she asked quietly, "Mama, are you and Daddy SEPARATED now?"

"Yes, my dear. We are because we live in two different homes," said Mama Bunny.

"Does that mean you are also DIVORCED now?" questioned Zoey.

"Yes. Because we will live in two different homes for a long, long time. For the rest of our lives."

Zoey's nose stopped twitching and her ears flopped down. She said softly, "That makes me SAD." A big tear rolled down her gloomy, furry face. "I know," said Mama Bunny soothingly. "It's okay to be sad. Sometimes I am sad, too. Over time, we will both be less and less sad about it," said Mama Bunny as she stroked Zoey gently.

As the bunny go-kart reached the Sunny Bunny School, Mama Bunny gave Zoey a hug and smiled, "TREASURE TIME!"

Zoey squeaked. Her eyes lit up and she gave a toothy grin. She opened her door and hop-hop-hopped into the Sunny Bunny School as she waved goodbye to Mama.

Zoey bumped into her friends and squeaked some more in delight. "EEK EEK EEK!" all the bunnies cried out. The bunnies then hop-hop-hopped into the large hall that was filled with sparkly balloons and mountains of ice cream lettuce and upside down carrots dipped in chocolate! Zoey and her best friend, Pixie, held paws and hop-hop-hopped over the shiny molehills and through the shimmering sand tunnels with all the other little bunnies.

"Pant! Pant! Pant!" huffed and puffed Zoey as she and Pixie sat down to take a rest. As they looked around with curiosity at all the twinkly colors in the room, Zoey's face drooped again and she felt her stomach pinch tight, "Do you know that my Mama and Daddy are SEPARATED now?" Zoey asked Pixie.

"No", replied Pixie, her eyes wide open. "Why are they SEPARATED?"

"I don't know", shrugged Zoey. "But it makes me sad." And her ears began to flop once more.

"Well, why don't you ask your Daddy?" suggested Pixie. "He's right there," as she pointed to the door.

"OOOOOH!!!" squeaked Zoey as she looked up and hop-hop-hopped over to Daddy. Usually she didn't see Daddy until the weekend, so she was very, very excited.

Daddy lifted Zoey up and they rubbed noses to say hello. Daddy had made a special trip to see his bunny on Treasure Hunt Day.

As Zoey sat in Daddy's lap, she rested her long, velvety ears on his shoulder and watched the other bunnies hop, hop, hop all over the room looking for treasures. She then gazed at the honey-mint pea drops dangling from the roof and quietly asked Daddy, "I'm CONFUSED. Why are you and Mama getting DIVORCED? Weren't you happy in one home?"

"I see there is a lot on your mind," replied Daddy. "Well Zoey, we were happy living together in one home for some years. But then we stopped being similar and slowly became different. Mama and I changed and began arguing more. We began to think and feel differently from each other," answered Daddy gently.

"I see," replied Zoey. But she really didn't. She was still very CONFUSED and now her stomach really hurt. She hopped off Daddy's lap and began searching for Pixie. All the bunnies were giggling in the huge, red tub of crimson and golden autumn leaves that were floating around, tickling their bellies and floppy ears. "Oooooh!" The Glittering Feather was hidden somewhere in the leaves. All the bunnies were hoping it would fly up and choose to tickle them!

Zoey decided to jump into the red tub and try her luck as well. Suddenly, Zoey felt a breeze inside her ear. She shook her long, velvety ears, as it was very, very ticklish. And then, she sneezed loudly, "AH-CHOOOO!" and the glittering feather flew out of her twitching nose! Zoey laughed and laughed as she held on tightly to the beautiful deep-blue feather covered in sparkles and pretty gems. The glittering feather swayed slowly in Zoey's hand as she beamed, "I'VE FOUND IT!"

With that, Zoey hopped out of the tub and sat by her friend Pixie so they could play with the glittering feather as it fluttered back and forth all by itself between them. As Zoey and Pixie were chatting, Zoey sighed to Pixie, "I still don't know why Mama and Daddy got divorced. It makes me so UNHAPPY and CONFUSED."

The wise old Fairy Owl with her golden beak, magic purple glasses, and feathers made up of hundreds of tiny sparkles, was sitting on top of the Egg Tree next to Zoey. Her tiny, sharp ears had heard exactly what Zoey had said. "You look mighty SAD and CONFUSED, Zoey," whispered the wise old fairy owl.

"Yes," sighed Zoey. "I am. My Mama and Daddy are SEPARATED and getting DIVORCED. I think it is MY FAULT. And—OUCH—my stomach hurts every time I think about it!"

"Your fault?" exclaimed the wise old fairy owl, her purple glasses glinting and her feathers dazzling. "How could it be your fault?"

"Well, I cried a lot when I didn't get to play outside with my friends," sighed Zoey. "I also didn't eat my greens and carrots the other day," whined Zoey, her ears all wilted. "And I am so, so messy. Mama and Daddy were always telling me to clean up, and I never, ever did." Zoey flopped on the floor with big tears rolling down her soft cheeks.

By this time Daddy had quietly come up behind Zoey and was listening to her BLAME herself. Daddy interrupted her, "It's NOT because of YOU Zoey. Our divorce has NOTHING to do with who you are or what you did." Daddy picked up Zoey and cuddled her on his lap. "It's because Mama and I CHANGED. We changed and became different in how we took care of the house, the garden, and each other. We changed on our own because sometimes grown-ups change in different ways and then do not get along as well."

"WHAT ABOUT ME?" squeaked Zoey, clutching her glittering feather that was squirming to soar to the top of the Egg Tree to join the wise old Fairy Owl. You see, the Glittering Feather came from the Fairy Owl!

Her eyes wide with fear, Zoey anxiously asked, "Are you going to change the way you will take care of ME?" She licked the chocolate covered carrot the Fairy Owl had just given her, to stop her tears.

"No, Zoey. We are NOT going to ever change the way we take care of you. We are still going to take care of you the best we know how. Mama is going to take care of you in her house and I will take care of you in my house." Then Daddy took a big lick of his ice cream lettuce.

"Does that mean I now have TWO HOMES?" asked Zoey, as chocolate dripped off her nose.

"Yes, it does. Many bunnies have one home with Mama and Daddy living together. Many bunnies also have two homes, one with a Mama and one with a Daddy."

"Hmmm..." said Zoey. Her eyes were suddenly glued to the hopping bunnies getting ready to catch the Magic Ball that could bounce eight feet high!

She suddenly felt a little better and her stomach hurt less because of what Daddy had told her.

The Head of School was getting ready to free the Magic Silver Ball. WHOOOOOOSH! The Magic Silver Ball flew out of her hand and began bouncing higher and higher all over the room. There were a stream of silver stars flowing behind it and squeaking, hopping bunnies with ears flapping and tails wiggling, leaping after it.

BOING! BOING! BOING! went the Magic Silver Ball. HOP! HOP! HOP! went the little bunnies. Suddenly Pixie, with her strong little legs took a flying leap into the air and caught the Magic Silver Ball with her teeth! "Hooray, Hooray!!" squealed Zoey, waving her Glittering Feather in the air. She was so happy for her friend Pixie. All the bunnies burst out clapping and the Head of School rang the Melting Rainbow Bell.

Warm fuzzy rainbows appeared all over the room. The Treasure Hunt was over and it was time to go home. "Bye, Daddy," whispered Zoey, as she rubbed noses with him. Zoey then hopped onto a rainbow, as did the other bunnies. Zoey's rainbow was red, orange, and yellow mixed together. As Zoey held on tightly to her rainbow, the rainbow gently floated off to the front of the Sunny Bunny School to find Mama waiting for Zoey.

"Look, Mama, look!!" Zoey grinned as she showed Mama the Glittering Feather.

"Ooooh, how exciting for you," replied Mama Bunny. "You are a lucky bunny, aren't you?" and she hopped on to the rainbow behind Zoey.

As the rainbow glided past the trees and whooshed over the bridges and ponds, Zoey happily said, "Daddy was at school today. He told me that I would have two homes. Does that mean my toys will be in two homes?"

"Yes, they will," answered Mama as the rainbow swerved to avoid Mr. Turtle on the path.

"And will I have two beds? One in your home and one in Daddy's home?" asked Zoey as she ducked to avoid the pine tree's branches.

"Yes, you will," said Mama, as the rainbow chugged up the Corn Hill.

"And will I have two Glittering Feathers? One in your home and one in Daddy's home?" asked Zoey, her eyes wide with excitement.

"Well, there is only one Glittering Feather, isn't there?" said Mama. "And I don't think the Glittering Feather would like to move from one house to another." The Glittering Feather swayed and shimmered in agreement.

"But I DON'T LIKE moving from one home to another either!" shouted Zoey as the rainbow glided to the front door of their house. "I don't like my family separated and I really don't like divorce!" Zoey ANGRILY hopped into the house and slammed the door shut! Zoey let go of the Glittering Feather and it floated gently up to the ceiling and rested on the candle chandelier.

"It's okay to be angry. Changes can be hard at first." Mama Bunny called out.

Zoey was sulking in her room. Her ears drooped all the way to the floor as she lay on her bed.

"How about a crystal bubble bath to make you feel better, Zoey?" encouraged Mama Bunny as she came into Zoey's room.

Zoey peeked out from under the blanket. "Hmmmm... a crystal bubble bath so I can get the answers to my questions," she thought to herself. Usually, the lilac crystal bubbles would allow a bunny to ask any question and show them the dream answer they wanted inside it. But this time, Mama Bunny was going to also help with the answer. Mama didn't want Zoey to imagine things that just wouldn't be.

"Yes," said Mama. "I will let you ask whatever questions you want as long as you let me guide the crystal bubbles."

"OK," agreed Zoey and hopped out of bed, her face cheering up a little. As she entered the bathroom, it filled with blue-purple steam and tiny, lilac bubbles appeared all over. She hopped into the tub and Mama Bunny began scrubbing Zoey's back.

Zoey reached out her hand and let one crystal bubble rest on her palm, which slowly grew in size so that they could see into it. Zoey quickly blurted out her first question, "Is it MY FAULT that Mama and Daddy

are in TWO HOMES?" As she gazed deeply into the lilac bubble, she saw Mama and Daddy in one home, and they were quarreling about different things—the house, the garden, and each other. She then saw herself curled up in her bedroom, trying not to listen to them. But she could hear them, and she felt scared and confused. Zoey began to feel sad again and her stomach felt a sharp ache.

She whispered into the crystal bubble, "Are Mama and Daddy going to stay divorced forever and ever? If I am really, really good and do my homework, clean my room, and eat my greens, won't they get back together and live in one home again?" As Zoey peered into the lilac bubble, she saw two homes. One home had Mama Bunny in it and the other home had Daddy Bunny in it. Then, she saw herself in both homes. She was actually SMILING and PLAYING!

Also, there was no fighting between Mama and Daddy, and her stomach was not hurting anymore. What a surprise!

At this point Mama Bunny softly said, "one more question, Zoey, and then it's time for bed."

Zoey scrunched her face and closed her eyes, "Will Mama and Daddy still love me and take care of me in two homes, just like they did when we were all living in one house before the family changed?" Carefully, Zoey opened her eyes wide and stared at the lilac bubble. In it she saw many different pictures: It was her birthday and she was having a huge bunny party at Daddy's house with lots of friends and cousins. Then she saw herself in Mama's home and it was the Grand Bunny Holiday and there were carrot cakes, balloons, and friends laughing and playing with her.

Zoey also saw herself being fed, bathed, and taken to school by Mama and Daddy in different bunny go-karts. Again, she was happy and her stomach didn't hurt anymore. Zoey let out a big sigh of relief and her eyes drooped with sleepiness. She was satisfied, at least for now.

Mama Bunny blew out the lilac bubble and bundled Zoey in a warm towel and took her to bed. Zoey was already half-asleep and beginning to dream of chocolate carrots, ice cream lettuce, glittering feathers, and magic silver balls. With that, Zoey fell asleep as Mama Bunny blew out the candle and kissed Zoey a lovely goodnight. But wise Mama Bunny knew Zoey would have plenty of questions and feelings the next day, and perhaps even for the whole year. But for now, Zoey felt better.

Can you think of other questions that Zoey might have for Mama and Daddy Bunny about SEPARATION and DIVORCE?

Process Questions for Adults to Discuss With Children

1. What does separation mean? Is separation forever?

2. What does divorce mean? Is divorce forever?

3. Was it my fault that my parents got separated/divorced?

4. Why do parents sometimes get separated/divorced?

5. Is it my job to make my parents live together?

6. If I work really hard and am really good, will my parents live together again?

7. How do I feel about my parents' separation/divorce?

8. How can I make myself feel better about my parents' separation/divorce?

9. Will my parents be nice to each other now that they are divorced?

10. Will I always have two homes?

11. How do I feel about moving between and living in two homes?

12. What does my "two home" calendar look like?

13. Can I take my clothes, shoes, toys and books back and forth between my two homes?

14. Will I have a set of toys, books, blankets and clothes I need in each home?

15. Will I be able to speak to my other parent when I am in one home?

16. Is it okay to miss a parent? What can I do if I am missing a parent?

17. Will my parents always love me and take care of me, like they have in one home?

18. Can I talk to my friends, family, teachers and parents about my thoughts and feelings about the separation/divorce?

19. Will I ever feel okay again?

20. Are there any other questions I can think of about separation/divorce and my parents?

Made in the USA
Middletown, DE
11 July 2019